UNFORCED
Rhythms of Grace

By

Pastor David Newell
Copyright © 2018

There is a great need today in the Body of Christ to understand the balance of Grace and Faith. For four years, I hosted "Ask the Pastor" on TCT TV . During that time our panel answered many questions people needed answers to and we were amazed by the lack of theological understanding in many of the questions. In order to dispel confusion and bring understanding to God's people, I have endeavored to put this small booklet together to help people with fundamental questions concerning God's Grace.

The format of this booklet is by questions and answers. I have adopted the old catechism method of teaching which we experienced on the "Ask the Pastor" program. I trust the Holy Spirit to illumine your mind to see and understand these great truths from God's Word.

Q- Does the Bible teach that our sins, past, present and future are forgiven?

A- Yes. Let us examine the word "eternal", in relation to our salvation. The first scripture we should look at is found in Daniel 9:24. It is prophetic of the coming Messiah and His work: "to finish the transgression, to make an end of sins, to make reconciliation for iniquity, to bring in everlasting righteousness."

What Jesus Christ accomplished happened once for all. Think about this: 2000 years ago, all our sins were future. Now let us look at Hebrews 5:9: "And having been perfected, He (Jesus) became the author of eternal salvation to all those who obey Him." We are saved for eternity and we are kept by God (John 6:37; 10:27-30; Jude 24; 1 Peter 1:5). Jesus doesn't get back on the Cross every time we sin: "not with the blood of goats and calves, but with His own blood He entered the Most Holy Place once for all, having obtained eternal redemption." (Hebrews 9:12).

The Lord wants us to get the picture that He deals in eternity: "And for this reason He is the mediator of the New Covenant, by means of death, for the redemption of the transgressions under the first covenant, that those who are called may receive the promise of "eternal inheritance" (Hebrews 9:15). As far as God is concerned, sin has been dealt with once for all: "But this Man, after He had offered one sacrifice for sins forever, sat down at the right hand of God' (Hebrews 10:12).

Now, we must understand the relation of our spirit, soul and body if we are to understand Hebrews 10:14 NKJV: "For by one offering, He has perfected forever those who are being sanctified". When we were born again, it was our spirit that was re-born and sealed. (Read Eph.4:24; Eph.1:13; 2 Cor.1;22). We will look at this correlation of spirit, soul and body (1 Thess.5:23) in a later question.

With this understanding, let's look once again at Hebrews 10:14 NKJV: "For by one offering He (Jesus) has perfected forever (in our spirit) those who are being sanctified (in our soul: mind, will and emotions). Our spirit is sealed and perfected. Our soul (mind, will and emotions) are being sanctified and renewed (Romans 12:1-2).

Q- How important is our knowledge of our spirit, soul and body, as it relates to our sanctification?

A- First, we must know we have been created in the image of God (Genesis 1:26). We are spirit beings. The Apostle Paul confirms this truth: "Now may the God of peace Himself sanctify you completely and may your whole spirit, soul and body be preserved blameless at the coming of our Lord Jesus Christ' (1 Thess.5:23). It is true that we are all born sinners (Psa.51:5) and had the nature of the devil working in us (Eph.2:2-3). But once we received salvation in Christ, we became a new person in the spirit (2 Cor.5:17). Our body did not change at salvation. Our soul (mind, will, and emotions) did not automatically change at that time either.

Our minds must be renewed daily. But our spirit has been changed and sealed forever. Most believers have been taught to believe that after salvation, they are still the same at the core (i.e they must always struggle with the old nature). They believe they have two natures but that division makes them nothing like Christ.

The Apostle Paul gives us the right understanding: "Shall we continue in sin that grace may abound?" (Romans 6:1). The first reason Paul gives us is "how shall we, that are dead to sin, live any longer therein" (Romans 6:2). Paul makes it clear we are baptized into Christ (Romans 6:3) and have experienced death to our old nature: "Or do you not know that as many of us as were baptized into Christ were baptized into His death?"

Yes, but Christians do sin (1 John 2:1-2), so how do we reconcile this? One reason we still sin is that we don't have a revelation of these truths: "And you shall know the truth, and the truth shall make you free." (John 8:32).

Our minds have been programmed (like computers in one sense). Because we were born in sin, our old sin nature(the old man) programmed our minds how to be bitter, unforgiving,angry and selfish. When we are born again, we become totally new in our spirits (2 Cor.5:17).

In our spirit, we are as pure and perfect as Jesus (1 John 4:17; 1 Cor.6:17; Eph.4:24).. Paul called this "resurrection life" (Roman 6:5). However, we must know something in order to experience this. Paul said, "that the body of sin might be destroyed, that henceforth we should not serve sin" (Romans 6:6). We are not "sinners saved by grace". We are New Creations in Christ. Our sin nature is dead and gone but it left behind a body of sin which is the carnal mind. For this reason, our mind must be renewed daily (Rom.12:2).

We must re-program our mind through God's Word as to who we are in the Spirit. Some teach that the old self (sin nature) is constantly being resurrected. There are no scriptures to cover that. Satan has no power to do that and Jesus never would. The old self left behind habits and ways of displaying our thoughts and emotions. When we sin it is because our mind has not been renewed, not because we have an old sin nature.

Some would say, "What's the difference? Whether it is my old nature or an unrenewed mind. I still struggle with the desire to sin?" There is a gigantic difference. If we still have an old sin nature, then we will live in spiritual schizophrenia (a divided mind). But if it is just our unrenewed mind that is causing us the difficulty, we know how to change it.

Think about it, if people retained a sin nature even after the new birth, then whatever sin bound you before salvation would still bind you after salvation. The testimony of millions have been they can't even relate to their old life or the persons that did those things, because they are new people with renewed minds (2 Cor.5:17).

Q- Why is it, I keep asking the Lord to do something for me, I don't get an answer?

A- There may be several reasons you are not seeing an answer to your prayer, but let's examine one reason in particular. Have you considered the Lord has already done everything for you that you would need: "Grace and peace be multiplied to you in the knowledge of God and of Jesus our Lord, as His divine power has given to us all things that pertain to life and godliness through the knowledge of Him who called us by glory and virtue." (2 Peter 1:2-3).

What we lack is knowledge. According to God's Word, I have already been healed (1 Peter 2:24). I already have the same power that raised Jesus from the dead within me (Eph.1:19-20; 2:6). We should never try to "get God" to heal us, rather stand on His finished work and give thanks. Note: Jesus gave thanks before the miracle of the loaves and the fishes(John 6:11,23). Do we need peace and joy? Rather than ask for it, give thanks it is already in your born again spirit (Gal.5:22-23). But you say, "I don't feel His love"?

Read Romans 5:5: "Now hope does not disappoint because the love of Christ has been poured out in our hearts by the Holy Spirit who was given to me." As a believer, you already have His love in your born again spirit. Once we get ahold of this revelation, we can stop striving. The devil can no longer condemn you for "not having enough faith"

Also, it breaks off of us a legalistic mindset that we have to earn things from God. Perhaps the reason the Lord has been silent toward you is that He has already provided what we need. What more can He say than "you have already got it. Where do we get that knowledge? It comes as we meditate on God's Word. We continue in 2 Peter 1:4: "by which have been given to us exceedingly great and precious promises (including healing, prosperity,blessing) that through these you may be partakers of the divine nature, having escaped the corruption that is in the world through lust." You say, "Well God's blessings are in Heavenly Places according to Eph.1:3 which says "Blessed be the God and Father of our Lord Jesus Christ, who has blessed us with every spiritual blessing in heavenly places in Christ." Yes, but let's keep reading.

Ephesians 2:6 tells us WE are seated with Christ in "heavenly Places", far above all principalities and powers. In addition, look at Philemon 6: "that the communication of your faith may become effectual (your faith will start to work) by the acknowledging of every good thing which is in you in Christ Jesus". Start acknowledging these good things, these promises, concerning who you are in Christ and what you already have in Him. Now your faith will begin to flourish.

People have already been saved (1 John 2:2) but they have to receive that salvation by grace through faith, as well as every other promise in the Word. Most believers know God can do all of these things, but they don't think He has already done anything yet. As a result, they start from the position of unbelief, rather than resting on what God has said He has already done (John 19:30).

Q- Can we excuse sin because we are under grace?

A- No. One of the aspects of grace is given to us in Titus 2:11-12 " For the grace of God that brings salvation has appeared to all men, teaching us that denying ungodliness and worldly lusts, we should live soberly, righteously and godly in the present age." When we come to the Lord for salvation, we confess our sin(literally hamartia, singular). What is that sin and the only one that would send us to hell? It is the sin of rejecting the conviction of the Holy Spirit to receive Jesus Christ as Lord and Savior (John 16:8-9).

Once we are saved, the Holy Spirit convicts and confirms to us the righteousness of Jesus Christ in our born again spirit that we are the righteousness of God in Christ (John 16:10; Romans 10:10). God's grace teaches us also that there are times we need to go to a brother or a sister and confess a trespass as it is often the doorway to healing(James 5:14-16). However, we must not become "sin-conscious": speaking of the sacrifice of Christ: "for then would would they not have ceased to be offered? For the worshippers once purified would have no more consciousness of sins."

The Lord wants us conscious of the righteousness of the Lord Jesus Christ. By the way, there is no way we can always confess our sins, as only the Holy Spirit can make us aware of what we need to confess. We tend to think of "big" sins and "little" sins but what if we just have not shown enough love or patience to a person?

We must let the Lord sort these things out. However, we should hold fast to 1 Corinthians 4:4-5: "For I know of nothing against myself, yet I am not justified by this, but He who judges me is the Lord. Therefore judge nothing before the time until the Lord comes, who will bring to light the hidden things of darkness and reveal the counsels of the hearts. Then each one's praise will come from God." We can be at rest in this one verse: "But if we walk in the light, as He is in the light, we have fellowship with one another, and the blood of Jesus Christ cleanses (continual present) us from all sins (1 John 1:7).

Q- Are you saying that because we live by grace (through faith), we don't have to live by the ten commandments?

A- The New Testament calls the Old Covenant and the ten commandments"the ministry of death"(2 Cor.3:7). It contrasts this with the phrase "the ministry of the Spirit"under the New Covenant (2 Cor.3:8). Read 2 Cor.3:9-18. Once we have been born again, God's laws have been written in our hearts by the Holy Spirit (Hebrews 8:7-12; 10:15-18). What are the commandments God writes in our heart? "And whatever we ask, we receive from Him because we keep His commandments and do the things that are pleasing in His sight. And this is the commandment that we should believe on the

Name of His Son Jesus Christ and love one another, as He gave commandment" (1 John 3:22-23).

Q- How do we live in the balance of grace and faith?

A- People often ask, "What do I need to do to receive the blessings of the Lord? "Many of these people point to their prayer life, their tithing record and their church attendance, and yet have not seen the answer to their prayers. The problem is they have believed receiving from the Lord is linked to their performance. Remember, grace means "unmerited, undeserved favor".

So we can say truthfully the good news is, grace has nothing to do with us. Grace is God's part.Faith is our positive response to what the Lord has already provided. Faith only appropriates what God has already provided for you. Faith is your part (Eph.2:8-9). Am important scripture to go along with this is found in Col.2:6 : "As you therefore have received Christ Jesus the Lord, so walk in Him. " We received the Lord by grace through faith.

Everything we receive from Him comes the same way. God's grace has already provided salvation for the whole world (Titus 2:11; 1 John 2:1-2). It was done 2000 years ago at Calvary. Your sins have already been forgiven. This is why Paul says "that if you confess with your mouth the Lord Jesus Christ and believe in your heart that God raised Him from the dead, you will be saved. For with the heart one believes unto righteousness and with the mouth confession is made unto salvation (Romans 10:9-10).

- We receive Christ's righteousness by faith rather than trying to produce our own righteousness (Phil.3:9).

- The word for "confess" in the Greek is homologeo which literally means "to assent, covenant, acknowledge". A true confession is not just mouthing words but should be heartfelt (Lk.6:46).

- The acknowledgment is also of Jesus Christ as God (1 Tim.3:16).

- True repentance is to turn wholly to Jesus in your heart and confession.

- Faith without works is dead (James 2:17). When you really believe in your heart, you will speak what you believe. Note Paul's confession of the power of grace and faith working in him (1 Cor.15:10).

Several years ago, while walking on beach in coastal North Carolina, the Lord taught me something. I stopped as the Lord told me to wait and observe something. I saw the tide move in and as it moved in, I watched a family of sandpipers run toward the incoming tide to receive their nourishment which came in with the tide.

The Lord asked me if I understood what I was seeing? Grace (the incoming tide brought the food) and Faith was demonstrated as the sandpipers did their part receiving the supply. Our part is to receive with thanksgiving what the Lord has already provided by grace. Many believers think that God moves sovereignly as He wills and when He wills. They believe God decides case by case, person by person,who will be healed and who will not be healed. But this is contrary to the Word. The scripture says Jesus came to destroy the works of the devil (Heb.2:14; 1 John 3:8).

The devil's work is to go about seeking whom he may destroy (1 Peter 5:8; John 10:10) God is being misrepresented. People blame the Lord for killing their family members, putting cancer on people to "teach them something". This is heresy. Putting on God what the devil is doing (John 10:10).

This is satanic deception. It makes people passive, adopting a "que sera sera" way of thinking. If you really believed God was trying to teach you something through putting sickness on you, then by all means don't go to your doctor. God is not responsible for killing babies, for rape, violence, poverty or sickness. Satan is the author of evil (Isa.5:20; Acts 10:38; Luke 13:10-16). God's will doesn't automatically come to pass. It is God's will that none should perish (2 Peter 3:9) but not everyone will accept what God has already provided through the death, burial and resurrection of the Lord Jesus (Matt.7:13).

Remember, it is not the truth that will set you free but it is the truth you know that will set you free(John 8:32). Grace without your positive response of faith won't save you and faith that isn't a response to God's grace will bring you into condemnation (1 John 5:4).

Q- How do we deal with the "fear of the Lord" from a New Testament, Grace perspective?

A- We can see the answer in a prophetic scripture concerning the Coming of the Lord Jesus Christ. "And there shall come forth a rod, out of the stem of Jesse, and a Branch shall grow out of his roots and the Spirit of the Lord shall rest upon Him, the spirit of wisdom and understanding, the spirit of counsel and might, the spirit of the knowledge and of the fear of the Lord" (Isa.11:2).

This is speaking of Jesus "fearing His Father". He did not dread His Father rather He honored, revered, trusted and submitted to His father. The early church walked in the fear of the Lord (Acts 9:31). We are speaking of the positive fear of the Lord (Psa.19:9). In many ways, America has drifted away from the fear of the Lord. Today, in many quarters, there is a total disregard for authority.

The Lord has made it clear from His Word that we must respect those in authority: police officers, government officials as well as pastors and ministers. Many have embraced a complete disregard for the rule of law. But God's Word will never change: "let every soul be subject unto the higher powers. For there is no power but God: the powers that be are ordained of God.

Whosoever therefore resists the power, resists the ordinance of God; and they that resist shall bring judgment on themselves" (Romans 13:1-2). Paul wrote this admonition when Nero ruled Rome and the world. He was one of the most corrupt rulers of all time. God acknowledged his rule, ensuring he would have a witness of the Gospel from Paul himself (Acts 23:11).

There is also a God-ordained church government "And He gave some, apostles, some, prophets, some, evangelists, some pastors and teachers, for the perfecting of the saints, for the work of the ministry, for the edifying of the Body of Christ." (Eph.4:11-12). In the same way, we are called to honor and respect natural governments, so we should give honor to church leaders (1 Tim. 5:17). James 3:16 says "for where envying and strife is, there is confusion and every evil work.' This is the opposite of the fear of the Lord and opens the door to sickness, disease, poverty, divorce and more. All leaders make mistakes and there is always room for improvement. (1 Tim.2:1-3). But they are still in a place of authority and when we honor them, we honor God. If after prayer and speaking respectfully to your leadership about your concerns and you still feel you are to leave, do it honorably.

That is what the early disciples did with the religious leaders over them (Acts 4:1-33). That is a godly attitude that is pleasing to the Lord. Romans 13:7-8 goes on to say, "render therefore to all their dues: tribute to whom tribute is due, custom to whom custom; fear to whom fear, honor to whom honor. Owe no man anything, but to love one another: he that loves another has fulfilled the law." People who won't pay their taxes are people who don't fear, respect or honor the Lord. However, if you are faced with compromising your beliefs or submitting to something that is wrong, then you must make a stand (Prov.29:25). When we fear man more than the Lord and His word, we do not fear the Lord. Finally, God will give you grace for all these things. He never commands us to do something without giving us enabling grace.

Consider this last admonition on this subject: "You shall not hate your brother in your heart. You shall surely rebuke your neighbor and not bear sin because of him" (Lev.19:17). This tells us not to be afraid of rebuking our brother, neighbor by telling him the truth. Do we love ourselves more than we love them? Are we not willing to suffer even a little rejection for righteousness sake? God's grace is there for us to fear, honor God more than man.

Q- Should I be concerned with "generational curses"? How does God's grace play a part in this issue?

A- Many Christians still hold to God's pronunciation to Moses, under the Law that He would visit the sins of the fathers to the third and fourth generation of those who hate Him(Ex.34:7). However, years later, the Lord gave a prophetic word through the prophet Ezekiel that plainly said the day would come when the father and the son would be responsible for just their own sins: "What do you mean when you use the proverb "the fathers have eaten sour grapes, and the children's teeth are on edge?" As I live, says the Lord God, you shall no longer use this proverb in Israel"

(Ezek.18:2-3). The Lord continues: "the soul who sins shall die. The son shall not bear the guilt of the father, nor the father bear the guilt of the son.

The righteousness of the righteous shall be upon himself" (Ezek.18:20). Finally, the last thing Jesus did on the Cross was to take the sour wine (sour grapes) (John 19:30). This ended the curse of the sins of the fathers being visited on the sons and succeeding generations. Galatians 3:13-14 puts the "frosting on the cake": "Christ HAS redeemed us from the curse of the law (all curses), having become a curse for us, for it is written cursed is every man that hangs upon a tree that the blessing of Abraham may come upon us.."

Q- How do we view Matthew 7:21-23 through the eyes of Grace?

A- Jesus made it clear that it is the doers of the Word that will enter the kingdom of heaven(James 1:22; 2:19-22). There are some people that just want the power of God, without a personal commitment to the Lord (Matt.7:22; Acts 19:13-16).

In contrast to the Matthew 7 verses, let's examine John 14:21-23: "He who has My commandments and keeps them, it is He who loves Me and he who loves Me will be loved by My Father, and I will love him and manifest Myself to him. If anyone loves Me, he will keep My word and My Father will love him, and WE will come to him and make OUR home with him". The balance of grace in this passage and in the Matthew 7 passages is found in Matthew 9:11-13; John 8:4-11; Romans 4:4-6,16; Gal.3:1-3,7,9-12; Eph.2:8-9; Titus 3:4-7).

The balance of grace and faith in responding to the Gospel is summed up in 1 Cor.15:10: "But by the grace of God I am what I am and His grace toward me was not in vain; but I labored more abundantly than they all, yet not I but the grace of God which was with me."

A sister verse to Matthew 7:21-23 is found in Luke 6:46: "But why do you call Me 'Lord,Lord' and not do the things which I say? "This tells us they probably did not do any of these "wonderful works" (prophecy, casting out demons,etc). They were deceived. They were ministering with their own abilities. It would be safe to say they were not born again believers who fell away and became reprobate. We base that on the John 14 verses. Matthew 7:23 tells us Jesus never knew them. In John 14:21-23, the person who by grace and faith accepted Jesus Christ as their Lord and Savior was known by Him. If you have the Holy Spirit, you are in the Kingdom of God (Romans 14:17).

Q- How does Isaiah 54:14-17 work in light of God's Grace in the New Covenant?

A- The Isaiah passage tells us that when we are established in righteousness, we will be "far from oppression" and we will "not fear" nor be "in terror". Under the New Covenant, we must understand it in the righteousness of Christ that makes all this happen" (Romans 5:17). "...much more they which receive abundance of grace and the gift of righteousness shall reign in life by One, Jesus Christ". Here we see that the "abundance of grace" is given to us when we were born again. As a result. We have the "gift of righteousness" as part of that grace package. This means we have " the Hope of Glory" on the inside,in our spirit, Jesus Christ. It is now Christ's righteousness that qualifies us. It is that same righteousness that Jesus spoke of in Matthew

6:33 that will cause the blessings of God's kingdom to flow to us.

<u>NOTES</u>

PASTOR
DAVID NEWELL

www.riverofliferaleigh.com

7 Fold ministry
Luke 24:30-35
Greet I am of Jesus

Luke 24:36-39
You recieve from the Lord when you
stay at peace
8 Whatever happens God has it
under control.... Lord I trust you
no matter what it is

1 Peter 5:6-9
This is how we stay at peace
Casting all your cares upon
him
How do we stay undevourable?
Cast our cares on Him!!!
He's a faithful God!! He will new
fail.(1) I am the Bread of life
John 6:51-56
John 15:7 bide in Him we'll get
If we abide in Him we'll get
our prayers answered
I am the light of the world
Free from Condemnation
John 8:10-12
You have been made worthy
through the blood of Jesus